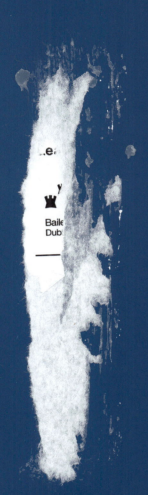

# Question & Answer ENCYCLOPEDIA

## AROUND THE WORLD

# Question & Answer

## ENCYCLOPEDIA

# AROUND THE WORLD

## Brian Williams

Miles Kelly
PUBLISHING

First published in 2004 by Miles Kelly Publishing Ltd
Bardfield Centre Great Bardfield Essex CM7 4SL

2 4 6 8 10 9 7 5 3 1

British Library Cataloguing-in-Publication Data
A catalogue record for this book is available from the British Library

ISBN 1-84236-421-9


Printed in China


**Publishing Director** Anne Marshall
**Senior Editor** Jenni Rainford
**Assistant Editor** Teri Mort
**Design Concept** John Christopher
**Designers** Jo Brewer, Debbie Meekcoms
**Cover Design** Debbie Meekcoms
**Picture Researcher** Liberty Newton
**Indexer** Helen Snaith
**Production Manager** Estela Boulton
**Colour Separation** DPI Colour Digital Ltd


www.mileskelly.net
info@mileskelly.net


All statistics used in this book are accurate at the time of going to press.

# CONTENTS

Where are Asia's high and low points?
Where is the world's largest desert?
Which is the most densely populated continent?
Where is the world's largest rainforest?
Where is the world's longest coral reef?
Where is the world's coldest place?
Which continent experiences extreme weather conditions?

Which country is also a subcontinent?
Where is Hanoi?
What is a zen garden?
Where do Sinhalese people live?

Why does Asia have some of the world's richest countries?
Where is the Forbidden City?
Why is Korea divided into North and South?
Which is the only city situated on two continents?
Who founded Singapore?

Which is Africa's largest city?
Which are Africa's most valuable minerals?
Which is the highest mountain in Africa?
How much of Africa is desert?
What is 'the smoke that thunders'?

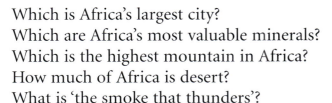

Who are the Zulus?
Where do the Masai people live?
What causes famine in some parts of Africa?
Why are Africa's game parks so important?
Which African leader fought for an end to apartheid?
Where is Timbuktu?

# **6** CONTENTS

Our world is a varied landscape with diverse countries and cultures. Mountains, rivers, deserts, seas, oceans, rainforests, grassland and extreme weather are just some of the Earth's features. For more than two million years humans have populated the Earth, building towns and cities to live in, and working the land to produce food and materials to sustain life.

↑ *Beaches in the Mediterranean are packed during the summer, when mostly European holidaymakers head for the sea.*

## Where are Asia's high and low points?

**Asia has the highest mountain on Earth, Mount Everest, and the lowest point, the Dead Sea.** In fact, the ten highest peaks (all more than 8,000 m high) are in the Himalayas, the greatest mountain range in Asia. But not all Asia is mountainous. There are huge areas of flat grasslands and desert, and the lowest point on Earth is the shore of the Dead Sea (in Israel and Jordan) – 400 m below sea level.

## Where is the world's largest desert?

**The world's largest desert is the Sahara, in northwest Africa.** The Sahara Desert covers an area of over 9 million sq km, stretching across the northern third of the African continent. It continues to grow as the areas surrounding it are overgrazed by animals and so turn to dust. Temperatures during the day can reach 50°C and yet drop to freezing during the night. Despite years without rain in the Sahara, certain animals and plants have adapted to be able to live in these conditions.

← *The Himalayan mountain range has formed over 25 million years, and continues to grow at a rate of 5 cm every year.*

## Which is the most densely populated continent?

**More than 700 million people live in Europe, which is only slightly bigger than Australia, making Europe the most densely populated continent for its size.** The most densely populated area stretches from southeast Britain, through northern France and into the Netherlands, where there are approximately 410 people per sq km. This figure is in vast contrast to a country such as the USA in North America, where there are about 27 people per sq km.

# Facts and statistics

### International organizations
Many countries of the world have joined together to create international organizations that provide law, order, aid and support throughout the world. These organizations use resources from the member states of the international community to help those in need, during periods of war or natural disasters. The United Nations (UN) is one such organization, set up in 1945 to try to resolve disputes between countries.

↑ *Red Cross workers travel around the world to regions of war, drought, famine or flood, to provide shelter, food and medicine for the victims.*

# Vital statistics

| | |
|---|---|
| Circumference | 40,075 km |
| Population | More than 6 billion |
| No. of countries | 194 |
| Largest continent | Asia – 17,400,000 sq km |
| Largest country | Russia, in Asia and Europe – 17,075,184 sq km |
| Highest mountain | Mount Everest, Asia – 8,863 m |
| Longest river | Amazon River, South America – 6,750 km |
| Largest lake | Caspian Sea, Asia – 371,000 sq km |
| Largest desert | Sahara Desert, Africa – 9.3 million sq km |
| Major religions | Christianity, Islam, Hinduism, Buddhism, Other – see page 33 for statistics |

## Where is the world's largest rainforest?

**The Amazon rainforest of Brazil, Peru and Bolivia, in South America, covers more than 6 million sq km.** It is home to more than 1,500 varieties of fish, more than 22,000 species of plants and a vast variety of insects, birds, reptiles and mammals. Local people and scientists use as many as 2,000 of the plant species found in the Amazon for use in medicine. Natural resources, such as gold, diamonds and rubber can also be found in the rainforest.

*Spider monkeys are just one of the many mammal species that are found in the Amazon rainforest.*

## Where is the world's longest coral reef?

**Covering more than 350,000 sq km, the Great Barrier Reef is found off the northeast coast of Australia.** More than 2,000 species of fish live among the many thousands of individual reefs, which are built from the remains of marine life. Some parts of the reef are up to 25 million years old.

*The Great Barrier Reef has been made a World Heritage Centre in order to protect it from pollution and damage caused by tourists and divers. Overfishing, mining, or tourists taking coral away from the Reef as a 'souvenir' of their trip, are some of the threats to the Reef.*

## Where is the world's coldest place?

**In July 1983, a record −89°C was recorded near the Vostok Scientific Station in Antarctica.** The average annual temperature on the continent is −57°C, and 98 per cent of the land is covered in ice, which accounts for 90 per cent of the world's ice.

## Which continent experiences extreme weather conditions?

**North America has some of the worst hurricanes, deepest snowfall and is home to one of the hottest places on Earth.** In 1998 Hurricane Mitch reached 290 km/h, killing 11,000 people and destroying more than 93,000 buildings. The greatest snowfall ever recorded was 11.5 m, measured in California in 1911. In contrast, Death Valley in California can reach a temperature of 57°C. Furthermore, an average of 800 tornadoes a year rage across U.S. states such as Kansas, Missouri, Iowa and Nebraska.

# Amazing **facts**

- The population of the world is estimated to grow at a staggering rate – approximately 360,000 babies are born every day.

- Approximately 150,000 people die every day.

- There are about 1,000 minor earthquakes every day, in various regions of the world.

- The Aral Sea, between Kazakhstan and Uzbekistan, is disappearing as a result of its water being used to irrigate crops. Today it is only one-third of its original size.

- Sweden in Europe has at least 90,000 lakes, which were formed during the last ice age, more than 100,000 years ago.

- In a region in northern Scandinavia, in Europe, it stays constantly light throughout summer, and constantly dark during winter.

- Maine is the first of the US states to see the sunrise each day.

- The Grand Canyon is the largest gorge in the world, at 349 km long.

- The highest temperature was recorded in 1922 in Libya, at 58°C in the shade.

- In the Nazca region of Peru, patterns have been scraped into the surface of the desert. They were created more than 2,000 years ago.

- There could be as many as 30,000 islands scattered around the Pacific.

- McMurdo is a community in Antarctica, which has cafés, a cinema and a church, for people visiting during the summer.

- The plates of the Earth's crust are moving the ocean floor at between 1.25 and 10 cm a year.

Asia is the world's biggest continent, both in land area and in the number of people who live there. It fills about one-third of the planet's land area. About six in every ten people on Earth are Asian. Asia's terrain is vast and varied and includes the world's highest mountain range, the Himalayas, as well as desert, steppe grassland, tundra, boreal (northern) forest and jungle.

### Which country is also a subcontinent?

**India is a subcontinent and is home to about one-fifth of the world's population.** The Indian subcontinent comprises India itself, which has more than one billion people, plus the countries of Pakistan, Bangladesh, Bhutan, Sri Lanka, Nepal and the Maldives. India also has 14 major languages and more than 400 other languages and regional dialects. Over the last 5,000 years the land has been invaded many times, and as migrating people have settled there a varied and diverse culture has emerged. India is now the world's largest democracy (see page 30) and has given rise to some of the world's most popular religions. The climate is hot and dry, but the monsoon season bring heavy rains and often flooding.

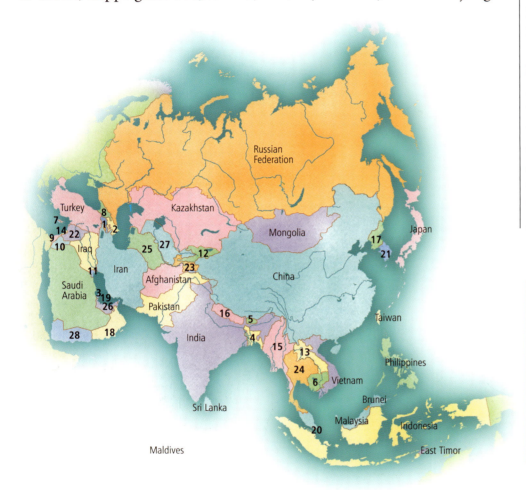

### map key

| | | | |
|---|---|---|---|
| 1 | Armenia | 15 | Myanmar (Burma) |
| 2 | Azerbaijan | 16 | Nepal |
| 3 | Bahrain | 17 | North Korea |
| 4 | Bangladesh | 18 | Oman |
| 5 | Bhutan | 19 | Qatar |
| 6 | Cambodia | 20 | Singapore |
| 7 | Cyprus | 21 | South Korea |
| 8 | Georgia | 22 | Syria |
| 9 | Israel | 23 | Tajikistan |
| 10 | Jordan | 24 | Thailand |
| 11 | Kuwait | 25 | Turkmenistan |
| 12 | Kyrgyzstan | 26 | UAE |
| 13 | Laos | 27 | Uzbekistan |
| 14 | Lebanon | 28 | Yemen |

## Facts and statistics

### United Arab Emirates (UAE)

The UAE is a federation of seven independent Arab states or emirates, the most well-known of which are Dubai and Abu Dhabi. An emirate is a region that is ruled by an emir or prince. About 96 per cent of the population are Muslim. Before the mid-1900s most Arabs made their living through pearl fishing or herding camels. Oil was discovered here in the 1950s, and by the 1970s the UAE had one of the world's richest economies.

⬆ *Bahrain's Emir is Sheik Isa bin Salman Al-Khalifa.*

## Vital statistics

| | |
|---|---|
| Area | 44,389,400 sq km |
| Population | More than 3.8 billion |
| Major cities | Kuala Lumpur (Malaysia), Mumbai (India), Seoul (South Korea) |
| Largest country | Russia* – 17,075,352 sq km |
| Highest mountain | Mount Everest – 8,848 m |
| Longest river | Chang Jiang – 6,380 km |
| Largest lake | Caspian Sea – 378,400 sq km |
| Largest desert | Arabian Desert – 1,250,000 sq km |
| Main religion | Islam – *c.* 807 million |

*\* Russia is partly in Europe: Asiatic Russia is 13,119,582 sq km*

↑ *Hanoi in Vietnam is modernizing rapidly, and its trade is increasing with Europe and the US. Traditionally, sampans, boats are used to transport goods to market.*

## Where is Hanoi?

**Hanoi is the capital of Vietnam, in Southeast Asia.** It is in the north of this long, narrow country. Ho Chi Minh City is the major city in the south. It used to be called Saigon until in 1976 it was renamed after Ho Chi Minh, who led North Vietnam in a long and bitter civil war against South Vietnam and their American allies.

## What is a zen garden?

**A zen garden is a simple outdoor space containing natural materials, neutral colours and clean lines designed to promote peace and serenity.** Zen is a form of Buddhism, which developed in China from about 500 AD. Zen Buddhism was introduced to Japan in about 1100 AD and became influential in Japanese culture and has since become very popular in western countries.

← *Zen gardens often contain one flower, such as a lotus, and small, pruned trees, such as bonsai.*

## Where do Sinhalese people live?

**Sinhalese people live in Sri Lanka, the island at the southern tip of the Indian subcontinent.** About 72 per cent of the population are Sinhalese, who are mainly Buddhist. The largest minority group in Sri Lanka are the Tamils who originated in southern India and are mostly Hindu. Sri Lanka was a British colony from 1802 until 1948 and was called Ceylon until 1972. Sinhalese and Tamil are the country's two official languages and tea is one of its most profitable exports.

↓ *Many Sri Lankan people are employed on plantations to pick tea leaves. Tea is one of Sri Lanka's main exports.*

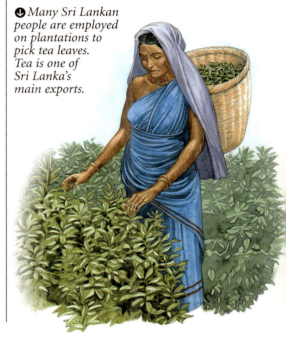

# Amazing **Asia**

- Russia is the largest country in the world, in land area, and is partly in Europe, partly in Asia.

- Japan and Indonesia are at risk from volcanoes. A ring of volcanoes called the Ring of Fire surrounds the Pacific Ocean.

- Asia has the world's largest bat, the Bismarck flying fox from Indonesia, and the smallest bat, Kitti's hog-nosed bat from Thailand.

← *In some parts of China, couples have been limited to having only one child in an attempt by the Chinese government to control population figures.*

- Garden plants native to Asia include tulips (Turkey) and rhododendrons (India).

- The Japanese call their country Nippon, meaning 'source of the Sun'. The red disc on the Japanese flag represents the Sun.

- The most common family name in the world is probably Zhiang – as many as one in ten Chinese people are called Zhiang.

- Temperatures in Asia can range from −68°C in Verkhoyansk, Russia, to 54°C in Tirat Zevi, Israel.

Asia was the home of great ancient civilizations, such as those of the Indus Valley and the Tigris-Euphrates region. The greatest imperial power in Asia was China, but by the 1800s much of Asia had come under European colonial rule. Japan was the first Asian country to 'westernize' its industries, and by the 1950s it had become one of the world's leading economic powers.

↑ *The Forbidden City in Beijing was once the emperor's private world, kept a secret from the people and foreigners. Beijing has been China's capital since 1421 when the emperor Yung Le made the city his base.*

## Why does Asia have some of the world's richest countries?

**Much of Asia's wealth comes from its manufacturing nations such as Japan, China, South Korea, Malaysia and India; and its oil-producers, such as Saudi Arabia, Brunei and Kuwait.** The manufacturing countries have large populations, many of whom work for low wages, so the average income per person is less than in Europe or North America. The oil-rich states have smaller populations, so average incomes are higher. The two richest rulers in the world are the King of Saudi Arabia and the Sultan of Brunei. The Middle East possesses more than 65 per cent of the world's oil reserves.

➲ *Oil has made some Asian countries, such as Kuwait, immensely wealthy.*

## Where is the Forbidden City?

**The Forbidden City is the old imperial section of Beijing, in China.** It forms a square that is surrounded by a moat and wall. Inside the boundaries are palaces that were once used by the Chinese emperors, but they are now open to the public as museums. Ordinary Chinese people and foreigners were once banned from entering the city. Only officials and nobles could gain entrance. One million workers took ten years to build the walled city, with its great halls, temples, pagodas and gardens.

# Asia **facts**

## Marco Polo and China

The Italian traveller, Marco Polo (1254–1324) wrote first-hand accounts of China that gave Europeans some of the first detailed reports about the Chinese way of life. After an long and intrepid journey from Venice, across Europe and Asia, Polo reached the palace of Kublai Khan (1216–94), founder of the Mongol dynasty in China, where he received a warm welcome.

➲ *When Marco Polo travelled to China, he wrote many books, such as* Description of the World, *in which he told of Kublai Khan's advanced society. His work also encouraged European interest in the east and may have motivated other explorers.*

◐ *Mahatma Gandhi led peaceful protests to campaign for India's independence. He saw this achieved in 1947, but was assassinated a year later by a fanatic of the Hindu religion.*

## Why is Korea divided into North and South?

**At the end of the Second World War (1945) Korea was occupied by Russia and America, who divided the country into communist North Korea and democratic South Korea.** Korea is a peninsula, or strip of land, on the east coast of Asia, bordering China. Its old name was Joseon. The Korean War (1950–53) failed to settle disputes, and the two Koreas remain separated by a heavily guarded border control.

● *Seoul in South Korea is a busy, modern city. South Koreans enjoy a much higher standard of living than people across the closely guarded border, in the North.*

● *Singapore skyscrapers rise from a small island linked to the mainland by a causeway.*

## Which is the only city situated on two continents?

**Istanbul, in Turkey, lies in both Europe and Asia.** It stands on both banks of the strait called the Bosporus, which separates the two continents. The Asian part of the city is one and a half times smaller than the European part. Istanbul had been called Byzantium and (from AD 330) Constantinople, and was the capital of the eastern half of the Roman Empire. It became Istanbul in 1453 when the Turks captured it.

## Who founded Singapore?

**Singapore was founded in 1819 by Sir Stamford Raffles.** He built a British trading base on what had been a small fishing village, which then flourished as a small republic at the tip of the Malay peninsula. It became a major port, and is now a busy trade centre. The people are mostly Chinese and Malay.

● *Istanbul is the gateway between Europe and Asia. Because the continents are joined, it is a super-continent known as Eurasia.*

# Key **dates**

| | |
|---|---|
| **c. 30,000 BC** | Stone Age people live in Asia. |
| **8000 BC** | First farm and towns form in Asia. |
| **3500–500 BC** | First writing in Sumer (Iraq); rise of first Asian empires (Assyria, Babylon, Persia). |
| **c. 1760 BC** | Shang dynasty founded in China. |
| **c. 660 BC** | Jimmu Tenno is first emperor of Japan. |
| **269 BC** | Asoka rules India. |
| **221 BC** | Shih Huangdi is first emperor to rule all China. |
| **c. 800 BC** | Khmer empire in Cambodia. |
| **AD 1096** | First Crusade (war for Holy lands) – the last one ends 1291. |
| **1200s** | Mongols conquer much of Asia. Marco Polo visits China. |
| **1299** | Ottoman empire founded in Turkey. |
| **1483** | Russians explore Siberia. |
| **1500s** | Regular trade contacts by sea with Europe. Mogul Empire in India. Japan united by Hideyoshi. |
| **1700s** | Britain and France fight for control of India. |
| **1800s** | China and Japan became open to western trade. |
| **1912** | China becomes a republic. |
| **1937** | War between Japan and China. |
| **1941–45** | Japan joins Germany and Italy to fight Allies in Second World War. |
| **1947** | Pakistan and India independent from Britain; Pakistan split into East and West Pakistan (Separation). |
| **1950–53** | Korean War. |
| **1964–73** | Vietnam War. |
| **1971** | East Pakistan becomes Bangladesh and West Pakistan becomes Pakistan. |
| **1980–88** | War between Iran and Iraq. |
| **1991–92** | War between Iran and Iraq. |
| **2003–04** | Iraq War fought between Iraq and the USA, UK and allies. |

Africa is a huge continent, covering about 20 per cent of the Earth's land surface. Only Asia is bigger. Africa comprises 53 different countries and more than 600 different tribal or ethnic groups. Africa's landscape is varied, with the world's largest desert, the Sahara, and the world's second longest river, the Nile. It has vast expanses of tropical grasslands or savanna, as well as rainforest.

## map key

| | | | |
|---|---|---|---|
| 1 | Benin | 11 | Liberia |
| 2 | Burkina Faso | 12 | Malawi |
| 3 | Burundi | 13 | Republic of Congo |
| 4 | Central African Republic | 14 | Rwanda |
| 5 | Djibouti | 15 | Senegal |
| 6 | Equatorial Guinea | 16 | Sierra Leone |
| 7 | Gambia | 17 | Swaziland |
| 8 | Ghana | 18 | Togo |
| 9 | Guinea-Bissau | 19 | Tunisia |
| 10 | Lesotho | 20 | Western Sahara |

## Which is Africa's largest city?

Cairo, in Egypt, is Africa's largest city, with more than 15 million people living there. It outranks other big cities in the continent, such as Algiers (Algeria), Lagos (Nigeria) and Johannesburg (South Africa). Like other cities of northern Africa, Cairo has Islamic mosques, open-air markets (bazaars) and tall, modern buildings. All over Africa cities are growing rapidly, as people leave the countryside to look for work in towns.

⊙ *Cairo has grown into a large, modern city, but old mosques (Muslim places of prayer) remain.*

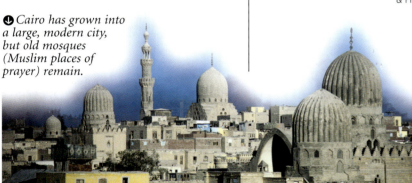

# Facts and statistics

### The Suez Canal

Completed in 1869, the Suez Canal soon became one of the world's largest artificial waterways. Before it was built, ships from Europe had to sail around Africa to reach East Asia. In 1956, the Egyptian government took control of the canal. Tolls paid by ships that use the canal provide a major source of income for Egypt.

➥ *The 165-km long Suez Canal runs from the Red Sea to the Mediterranean Sea, linking Europe to India and East Asia.*

# Vital statistics

| | |
|---|---|
| Area | 30,303,000 sq km |
| Population | More than 840 million |
| Major cities | Algiers (Algeria), Cairo (Egypt), Casablanca (Morocco), Johannesburg (South Africa), Lagos (Nigeria) |
| Largest country | Sudan – 2,505,5810 sq km |
| Highest mountain | Mount Kilimanjaro, Tanzania – 5,895 m |
| Longest river | River Nile – 6,670 km |
| Largest lake | Lake Victoria – 69,484 sq km |
| Largest desert | Sahara Desert – 9 million sq km |
| Main religion | Christianity – c. 350 million |

## Which are Africa's most valuable minerals?

Gold, diamonds, coal, oil and gas are among the many valuable minerals that are mined in various parts of Africa. South Africa is mined for gold, diamonds, coal and cobalt. Algeria, Libya and Nigeria provide oil and gas. Diamonds are mined in Sierra Leone and copper is found in Zambia. Africa also produces iron ore, tin, bauxite (aluminium ore) and manganese.

## Which is the highest mountain in Africa?

At 5,895 m high, Mount Kilimanjaro, a dormant volcano in Tanzania, is the highest mountain in Africa. It is so high that, even though it is very near the Equator, its peak is always snow-covered. Its name in Swahili is *Uhuru*, which means 'freedom'.

*This section of the Victoria Falls is called the Devil's Cataract. The falls were named after Britain's Queen Victoria by 19th-century explorer David Livingstone, who travelled across much of Africa, and mapped out various parts of the continent.*

## How much of Africa is desert?

About 40 per cent of this hot continent is desert. The Equator crosses the middle of Africa and in most places it is hot all year round. There are great rivers and lakes in Africa but, in contrast, large areas of it are very dry and this has led to the spread of deserts. The Sahara is the biggest desert in the world, and stretches across north Africa. In the southwest of Africa are the smaller Namib and Kalahari deserts.

*Mount Kilimanjaro rises above the savanna in northern Tanzania, close to the Kenyan border. It formed over one million years ago.*

## What is 'the smoke that thunders'?

Victoria Falls is Africa's most famous waterfall and its African name Mosi-oa-tunya, means 'smoke that thunders'. This refers to the cloud of spray that rises above the Victoria Falls as the Zambezi River tumbles over a sheer rock wall. The rumble of the falls can be heard far away and sounds like distant thunder. The falls are 108 m high and 1,500 m wide.

*African athletes, especially those from the highlands of Ethiopia and Kenya, dominate world athletics in the long-distance events with their speed and agility.*

# Amazing **facts**

- Approximately half the population of Africa is under the age of 15.

- Liberia was founded as a land for freed African slaves from the USA.

- Fossils found in Africa's Great Rift Valley show that humans originated in Africa.

- Millet is an important crop in much of Africa. The seeds are ground into flour to make flatbread or a kind of porridge.

- When European leaders split the countries of Africa between them, only Ethiopia and Liberia remained independent and ruled by Africans.

- The world's biggest gold-field is in the Witwatersrand in South Africa.

By 1900 Africa was almost completely colonized by European countries. The colonial boundaries became the boundaries of new independent African nations, as African peoples sought self-government from the 1950s. Libya was the first African country to win its independence in 1951. In South Africa, the white minority controlled the government until the 1990s, under a system known as apartheid.

⬆ *A Zulu from South Africa wears traditional warrior dress, comprising of a short spear, or assegai, and an ox-hide shield. A regiment of Zulu soldiers is known as an impi.*

## Who are the Zulus?

**The Zulus are a people who live in South Africa.** In the early 1800s, they were a small tribe, mainly cattle-herders, but a chief named Shaka led a powerful army to fight against the Boers (Dutch settlers) who were taking their land. In 1879, the Zulus were defeated by the combined armies of the Boers and British in the Zulu War. Today the Zulus are citizens of the Republic of South Africa.

## Where do the Masai people live?

**The Masai are a tribal group of people in Kenya, East Africa.** Traditionally, they lived as cattle-herders. Masai men were famous for their skill at hunting lions, armed only with spears. Many African countries have a mixture of tribal groups. There are about 50 ethnic groups in Kenya alone, including the Kikuyu, who are the biggest tribe.

## What causes famine in some parts of Africa?

**Famine can be caused by drought or civil war.** The regions hit hardest by drought include Ethiopia, Chad and Mali, which may go for a year or more without rain. Farmers rely on the seasonal rains to make their crops grow and so the lack of rain means that the soil becomes dry and vegetation dies. This leaves the local population with very little to eat. Civil wars are also responsible for famine because they disrupt farming and trade, thus increasing the risk of famine in some areas.

⬆ *Masai women wear colourful headbands and beaded collars for tribal ceremonies. Many other traditional African costumes are now seldom seen except for tourist displays.*

# Africa **facts**

## Key **dates**

| | |
|---|---|
| 900 BC | Kingdom of Kush founded. |
| 100 BC | Niger-Congo languages spread from West Africa to other regions. |
| AD 641 | Invading Arabs introduce Islamic faith. |
| c. 1000 | The kingdoms of Benin and Ife are created. |
| 1100 | Great Zimbabwe culture founded in southeast Africa. |
| 1450 | Portuguese develop trading posts in parts of Africa. |

| | |
|---|---|
| c. 1510 | First African slaves taken to USA. |
| 1652 | Dutch set up colony in South Africa. |
| 1795 | British take Cape Colony from Dutch. |
| 1835 | Boers (Dutch settlers) set off on Great Trek from the Cape. |
| 1847 | Liberia becomes independent. |
| 1869 | Suez Canal is opened. |
| 1879 | The Zulus are defeated by the British and Boer armies. |
| 1884 | Africa is divided between European leaders. |

| | |
|---|---|
| 1889 | Boer War break out in South Africa. |
| 1902 | British defeat the Boers to seize their lands as part of the British Empire. |
| 1948 | Apartheid begins in South Africa. |
| 1951 | Libya becomes indepedent. |
| 1957 | Gold Coast independent from Britain, as Ghana. Many colonies become independent over the next 15 years. |
| 1963 | Organization of African Unity formed. |
| 1994 | Nelson Mandela elected South Africa's first black president. |

## Which African leader fought for an end to apartheid?

**Nelson Mandela was imprisoned for 26 years for campaigning for the end of apartheid.** Apartheid was a social system in place in South Africa that separated black and white citizens. Mandela was jailed in 1964 for being a senior member of the ANC (African National Congress). In 1990, South African president, F. W. de Klerk, released Mandela.

*➜ Mandela became the first black president of South Africa in 1994. Under his leadership, apartheid gradually began to break down.*

## Why are Africa's game parks so important?

Tourism is a major source of income for African countries, as tourists flock to the game parks to see the amazing variety of wildlife. Lions, giraffes, rhinos, elephants, hippos, antelope and many more animals are found in game reserves across Africa. The reserves protect the animals from poachers, who shoot elephants for their ivory tusks and rhinos for their horns. People used to go to Africa on safari to shoot 'big game', but now many of these animals have become endangered and so are protected inside game parks, such as the Kruger in South Africa and the Tsavo in Kenya.

*➜ Big cats, such as the cheetah, can be spotted by tourists travelling through game reserves in South Africa, Tanzania and Kenya.*

## Where is Timbuktu?

**Timbuktu is an ancient trading city south of the Sahara Desert in the African country of Mali.** The name means 'place of Buktu'. According to legend, a slave named Buktu was left there to guard her master's goods. Timbuktu was once rich and prosperous, a stopping place for camel travellers crossing the Sahara, carrying gold and salt. It later fell on hard times.

*⬅ Many people in Timbuktu live in traditional mud-brick houses.*

*⬅ This sculpture of the Sphinx was relocated to avoid damage when the Aswan Dam was built and the Nile was flooded. The 1,951-m long Aswan Dam was built across the River Nile in 1902. The Nile flows through the countries of Uganda, Sudan and Egypt, providing water for farming, fishing, homes and industry.*

*➜ The San people, or Bushmen, are hunters and gatherers who live in the Kalahari Desert. They collect honey from wild bees' nests, and bee grubs are considered a delicacy. They live and work in small, close communities. They were originally nomadic, moving around the country in order to search for food and to hunt animals. But today they usually settle in one area.*

Europe is the smallest continent, not counting Australia, and the most densely populated. It has the longest coastline of all the continents (more than 60,000 km), with mountains in the north and south enclosing a central plain. There are 42 independent countries in Europe, some are large (Russia, Ukraine, France and Spain) and others, such as Liechtenstein, are tiny.

## Where does Europe end?

**Europe has sea on three sides (north, west and south), but it merges with the Asian landmass on the eastern side.** There are natural land barriers forming a boundary between Europe and Asia. These boundaries include the Ural Mountains and the Caspian Sea, in Russia. Europe is separated from the continent of Africa by the Strait of Gibraltar, which lies between Morocco in Africa, and Spain in Europe.

## Where is Scandinavia?

**Scandinavia is the region of northern Europe with a shared geography and history.** The countries of Scandinavia are Norway, Sweden, Denmark, Finland and Iceland, which is an island in the Atlantic Ocean. The Scandinavian countries are famed for their landscapes of fjords (Norway), lakes (Sweden), forests (Finland), busy fishing ports (Denmark) and hot springs (Iceland).

## map key

| | | | |
|---|---|---|---|
| 1 | Albania | 9 | Lithuania |
| 2 | Andorra | 10 | Luxembourg |
| 3 | Belgium | 11 | Macedonia |
| 4 | Bosnia-Herzegovina | 12 | Moldova |
| 5 | Croatia | 13 | Netherlands |
| 6 | Estonia | 14 | Slovenia |
| 7 | Latvia | 15 | Switzerland |
| 8 | Liechtenstein | 16 | Yugoslavia |

# Facts and statistics

*Denmark's flag is Europe's oldest national flag, first flown in 1219. The Danish king at the time is said to have seen a white cross in a red sky before winning a battle.*

*Sweden, like all other Scandinavian countries, has an off-centre cross on its flag, based on the same legend as Denmark's flag. Sweden's flag may date back to 1449.*

*The white cross on the Greek flag represents the Christian faith. The blue represents the sea and sky, and the white symbolizes the people who fought for Greece's independence in the early 19th century.*

# Vital statistics

| | |
|---|---|
| Area | 10,534,600 sq km |
| Population | More than 700 million |
| Major cities | Berlin (Germany), London (UK), Madrid (Spain), Milan (Italy), Moscow (Russia), Paris (France) |
| Largest country | Russia – 4.7 million sq km (European area only) |
| Highest mountain | Mount Elbrus, Russia – 5,633 m |
| Longest river | Volga River, Russia – 3,531 km |
| Largest lake | Caspian Sea, Russia  – 438,695 sq km |
| Main religion | Christianity – c. 552 million |

⬆ *St Petersburg is Russia's second largest city, and boasts the world's biggest art gallery, the Hermitage Museum (shown above) and a famous opera and ballet theatre.*

## Which is the biggest country in Europe?

**Russia is so big that it is shared between Europe and Asia, so strictly speaking only part of Russia is 'European'.** Even so, at 4.7 million sq km, the European region of Russia is seven times bigger than the next biggest country in Europe, the Ukraine. Next come France, Spain and Sweden.

## How many countries make up the British Isles?

**The British Isles is made up of two independent countries: the United Kingdom and the Republic of Ireland.** The United Kingdom consists of Great Britain (the island containing the nations of England, Scotland and Wales) and Northern Ireland (part of the island of Ireland).

## Where do people walk on land that was once sea?

**The Netherlands.** The name Netherlands means Low Countries, and this region is very low-lying. Sea walls or dykes have been built to stop the sea flooding the land, and water has been pumped from flooded parts to turn salt marshland into fertile agricultural land. The reclaimed land is known as polders. About 40 per cent of the country has been reclaimed from the sea and 25 per cent of this is used for housing and roads. It takes about eight years after draining the land for it to be suitable for farming and building on.

➔ *Merchants built the network of over 100 canals that cross the Dutch city of Amsterdam.*

⬆ *The Tower of London is in the capital city of England. Building of the Tower was begun by William the Conqueror in 1078, when London was already 1,000 years old.*

⬆ *The Alps is the highest mountain range in western Europe, running through southeastern France, Switzerland, Italy and Austria. The range started to form more than 15 million years ago.*

## Amazing Europe

- Less than 3 per cent of mountainous Norway is cultivated.

- The UK is Europe's biggest island, at 229,850 sq km.

- The highest volcano in Europe is Mount Etna in Sicily, at more than 3,300 m.

- Turkey and Russia are each situated partly in Europe and partly in Asia.

- The highest peak in the Alps is Mont Blanc, at 4,807 m, but Mount Elbrus in the Caucasus mountain range is even higher, at 5,633 m.

Europe was the birthplace of ancient Greek and Roman culture, and later European ideas and technology were spread by explorers, traders and empire-builders to other continents. Europe was the first continent to undergo the Industrial Revolution, in the 1700s. It was also the cradle for two terrible world wars, 1914–18 and 1939–45. Since 1950, the European Union has become the dominant economic force in Europe.

⬆ *The Rock of Gibraltar is a 426-m high mass of limestone. Gibraltar was once an important naval base, but is now a favourite tourist location.*

## In which city is the Kremlin?

The Kremlin is the medieval centre of Moscow, which is the capital of Russia, and used to be the home of the Russian tzar (**emperor**). The name kremlin means fortress, and the first wooden fortress was built on this spot more than 800 years ago. The walls now in place date from the 1400s. Cathedrals and palaces were built around the Kremlin fortress. In 1917, the Kremlin became the headquarters of the world's first communist government, which then collapsed in 1991.

⬅ *St Basil's Cathedral, with its cluster of domes, is one of Moscow's landmarks.*

## Where is the Rock of Gibraltar?

Gibraltar is a rocky landmark at the southern tip of Spain, at the point where the Mediterranean Sea and Atlantic Ocean meet. About 30,000 people live there. The Rock (as Gibraltar is known) was held by the Arab and Berber Moors and the Spaniards until 1713, when it was ceded to Britain by treaty. Spain wants Gibraltar back, but local people voted to stay British.

➡ *The colony of Gibraltar is represented by this flag and covers an area of 6.5 sq km.*

# Europe **facts**

## Key **dates**

| | | | |
|---|---|---|---|
| **c. 8000 BC** | End of last ice age. | **1066** | The Normans conquer England. |
| **4000 BC** | Farming reaches northern Europe. | **1236–41** | Mongols invade Russia. |
| **2000 BC** | Minoan civilization on Crete. | **1300** | Renaissance (re-birth in the arts) begins in Italy. |
| **c. 480 BC** | Hunters mark out territories; Celts spread. Greece at peak of power. | **1338** | Black Death (bubonic plague) hits Europe. |
| **AD 50** | Rome is world's biggest city (one million people). | **1400s** | Portuguese start overseas exploration. |
| **285** | Roman Empire splits in two. | **1700s** | Industrial Revolution begins in Britain. |
| **476** | Collapse of western Roman Empire. | **1804** | Napoleon becomes emperor of France. |
| **711** | Spain invaded by Moors. | | |

| | |
|---|---|
| **1871** | Germany united. |
| **1914–18** | First World War. |
| **1939–45** | Second World War. |
| **1957** | European Economic Community (now European Union) set up. |
| **1961** | Berlin wall is erected, dividing Germany. |
| **1990** | Collapse of Communism in Eastern Europe. Collapse of Berlin Wall reunites Germany. |
| **2004** | Expansion of EU to 25 member states. |

➡ *Some members of the European Union have discussed the creation of a European federal state, represented by the current European Union flag. However, most member states prefer their national independence and wish to keep their own flags and currencies.*

⬇ *The Colosseum in Rome is the biggest Roman amphitheatre (open-air arena): 49 m high and 157 m across. Inside there was room for 80,000 spectators.*

## Which is Europe's smallest country?

Europe's, and the world's, smallest independent state is the Vatican City, official home of the Pope (the head of the Roman Catholic Church). Fewer than 1,000 people live in the Vatican City. It has its own police and the Pope's bodyguard force, the Swiss Guard, who wear traditional uniforms. It also has a national anthem, stamps, coins, flag and a radio station.

⬇ *The Vatican's main buildings are St Peter's (shown below), one of the world's largest churches, and the Vatican Palace.*

## How did the European Union begin?

The European Union evolved from a series of economic agreements, such as the common market, set up by various European nations, from the 1950s. The founder members of the EU were France, Germany, Italy, Netherlands, Belgium and Luxembourg. More countries joined and by 2004 the EU had 25 member-states and its own parliament. A common currency (the euro) is shared by some member states.

## Which European city was once the heart of the Roman Empire?

The city of Rome, in Italy, was once the heart of the Roman Empire. The Romans conquered most of Europe over 2,000 years ago, and imposed their laws and culture on the peoples who lived under their rule. This had an enormous effect on later European history. The remains of some buildings from ancient Rome, such as the Colosseum and the Pantheon, still stand today in Rome, the capital of Italy.

⬅ *The flag of Portugal dates from 1910. The shield in the centre dates from the 12th century, and the nautical instrument behind it celebrates Portugal's exploration and maritime past.*

⬅ *The Swiss flag, which dates from the 14th century, is the only other completely square flag (the other is the flag of the Vatican City). In honour of its founder, Swiss, Jean Dunant, the flag of the International Red Cross organization is a red cross on a white background, the reverse of the Swiss flag.*

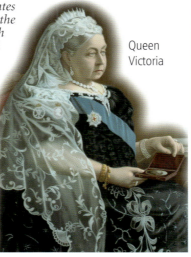

Queen Victoria

# European **rulers**

**Queen Victoria of Britain** – Longest reign in Britain of 63 years (1837–1901).

**Queen Elizabeth, the Queen Mother** – (1900–2002) The first member of the British royal family to reach the age of 100.

**Louis XIV of France** – One of the longest reigns in European history, of 72 years.

**Louis XIX of France** – Shortest reign (15 mins, before abdicating in 1830).

The third largest continent, North America extends from Greenland and Alaska in the Arctic north, through Canada and the United States, to Mexico in the south and the islands of the Caribbean Sea. The landscape of North America includes bleak polar regions, towering mountain ranges such as the Rockies, vast grassy plains or prairies (now ploughed for cereal crops), forests, mighty rivers and the Great Lakes.

## US states

| | | |
|---|---|---|
| Alabama | Louisiana | Ohio |
| Alaska | Maine | Oklahoma |
| Arizona | Maryland | Oregon |
| Arkansas | Massachusetts | Pennsylvania |
| California | Michigan | Rhode Island |
| Colorado | Minnesota | South Carolina |
| Connecticut | Mississippi | South Dakota |
| Delaware | Missouri | Tennessee |
| Florida | Montana | Texas |
| Georgia | Nebraska | Utah |
| Hawaii | Nevada | Vermont |
| Idaho | New Hampshire | Virginia |
| Illinois | New Jersey | Washington |
| Indiana | New Mexico | West Virginia |
| Iowa | New York | Wisconsin |
| Kansas | North Carolina | Wyoming |
| Kentucky | North Dakota | |

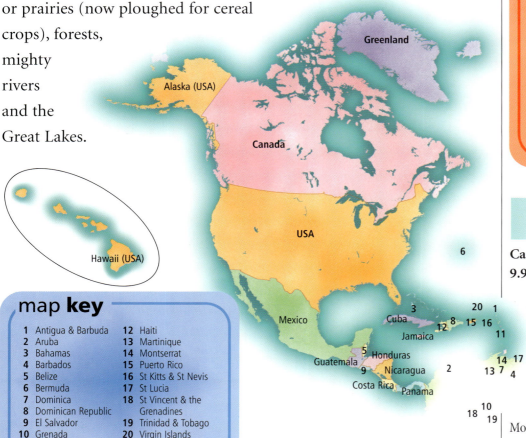

## map key

| | | | |
|---|---|---|---|
| 1 | Antigua & Barbuda | 12 | Haiti |
| 2 | Aruba | 13 | Martinique |
| 3 | Bahamas | 14 | Montserrat |
| 4 | Barbados | 15 | Puerto Rico |
| 5 | Belize | 16 | St Kitts & St Nevis |
| 6 | Bermuda | 17 | St Lucia |
| 7 | Dominica | 18 | St Vincent & the |
| 8 | Dominican Republic | | Grenadines |
| 9 | El Salvador | 19 | Trinidad & Tobago |
| 10 | Grenada | 20 | Virgin Islands |
| 11 | Guadaloupe | | |

### Which is North America's largest country?

**Canada, with an area of more than 9.97 million sq km, is North America's largest country.** The United States is a little smaller, at 9.37 million sq km, but the population of Canada is only 11 per cent of that of the USA. Canada shares a 6,400 km long land border with its southern neighbour, the USA. The Rocky Mountains stretch almost 5,000 km southwards from Canada, south into the United States.

# Facts and statistics

### The Rocky Mountains

Thousands of visitors flock to the Rocky Mountain range each year to see the vast array of fauna and wildlife, such as bears, deer, mountain lions, squirrels and minks. The Rockies stretch more than 4,800 km from Alaska to New Mexico. In the Canadian Rockies, the snow-capped mountains reach more than 3,600 m above sea level and the tallest peak is Mount Robson, at 3,954 m high. The Rockies are also a good source of lead, coal, silver and zinc.

*The brown grizzly bear once roamed much of North America, but is now less common. The biggest bears live on Kodiak Island, Alaska.*

# Vital statistics

| | |
|---|---|
| Area | 23,497,000 sq km |
| Population | 505 million |
| Major cities | Chicago (USA), Mexico City (USA), New York (USA), Philadelphia (USA), Toronto (Canada) |
| Largest country | Canada – 9,976,162 sq km |
| Highest mountain | Mount McKinley – 6,194 m |
| Longest river | Mississippi – 3,779 km |
| Largest lake | Lake Superior – 82,103 sq km |
| Largest US state | Alaska – 1.5 million sq km |
| Main religion | Christianity – c. 250 million |

⬆ *Red rocks rise hundreds of metres out of the otherwise flat Monument Valley, which is situated in both Utah and Arizona.*

## Why is the USA called the land of the skyscraper?

**The USA is home to some of the world's greatest cities, and many of the world's tallest buildings.** In many US cities, such tall buildings create dramatic skylines, particularly in Chicago, along the shore of Lake Michigan and in New York City, on Manhattan Island. Chicago once boasted America's tallest building, the Sears Tower, which has 110 floors and stands 1,707 m high with its topmost masts.

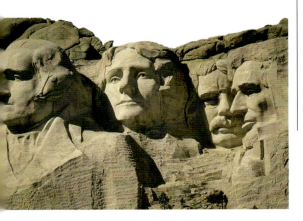

## Where is Monument Valley?

**Monument Valley is in the dry, western American state of Utah but also crosses into Arizona.** In the valley can be found some of the most spectacular scenery in the United States. Over thousands of years, the huge crags of sandstone have been eroded by the wind and rain, making the valley an ideal location for shooting 'western' films.

## Where are four presidents cut into stone?

**In the Black Hills of South Dakota, in the midwest United States.** A sculptor named Gutzon Borghum carved the heads of four US Presidents into the granite rock of Mount Rushmore. Each head is about 18 m high and can be seen from almost 100 km away. Work started on the monument in 1927 and lasted until the 1960s.

⬅ *The four presidents on the Mount Rushmore National Memorial are (left to right): George Washington, Thomas Jefferson, Theodore Roosevelt and Abraham Lincoln.*

⬆ *The Niagara River tumbles into a gorge. Spray and foaming water rise into the air, often forming rainbows.*

## Where are the Niagara Falls?

**There are two falls on the Niagara River: the Horseshoe Falls on the Canadian side and the American Falls on the US side.** The Horseshoe Falls are 792 m wide and 51 m high. The American Falls are 305 m wide and about 54 m high. The most water (about 85 per cent) crashes over the Horseshoe Falls. Each year millions of tourists head for Niagara Falls, which have been an attraction ever since European explorers first saw them in the late 1600s.

# Amazing **facts**

⬆ *Bridalveil Fall has a 436 m high drop and is the first waterfall seen by visitors to Yosemite National Park.*

- The Big Muddy is the name given to the Missouri, the second longest river in North America. It carries with it huge quantities of mud.

- The most important waterway in North America is the St Lawrence Seaway. Ships use it to move inland for 3,500 km from the Atlantic Ocean to the Great Lakes.

- This highest waterfall in the USA is the Yosemite Falls, Yosemite National Park, California, at 739 m high.

- North America's hottest spot is Death Valley, California, where a temperature of 57°C was recorded in 1913.

⬆ *Toronto is Canada's biggest city. Canada has far fewer people than the USA – 31 million compared to the USA's 287 million.*

North America includes countries with diverse cultures and traditions. Canada and the United States have historic ties with Britain, but Canada also has a large French-speaking minority. Both countries have populations of Native Americans, who retain many of their traditional cultures and languages, as well as people of African, Asian and European origin. In Mexico, people speak Spanish – this is also a legacy of the country's past.

## Who were the first Americans?

**The first people to live in North America were the Native Americans and Inuit, whose ancestors came from Asia, probably before the last ice age.** When Europeans invaded in the 1500s, the natives fought a fierce battle to keep their land. However, today Native Americans form less than one per cent of the population of the USA. Most Americans today are those whose ancestors came from Africa, Asia and Europe.

⬇ *Today, about one-fifth of Native Americans live on land known as reservations, which has been given back to them by the government.*

## Who were the Aztec and Maya?

**The Aztecs were a native people living in what is now Mexico, around 1300 AD: the Maya were a native people living in Central America around the same time.** The Aztecs built a city called Tenochtitlán,

⬆ *Chichén Itzá is an ancient sacred site of the Maya of Central America. The Maya people built stepped-pyramid temples in their cities.*

upon which Mexico City now stands. The Aztecs were conquered by the Spaniards in 1521, who destroyed their temples. Each of the Mayan Kingdoms had a capital city that was built entirely from stone.

# North America **facts**

## Key **dates**

| | |
|---|---|
| **c. 30,000 BC** | First hunters arrive from Asia. |
| **c. 10,000 BC** | People spread south across North America. |
| **AD c. 250** | Mayan culture in Mexico. |
| **c. 500** | Farming in Mississippi region. |
| **c. 900** | Caribs conquer Arawaks in the Caribbean. |
| **c. 950** | Toltec culture in Mexico. |
| **1000** | Vikings reach North America. |

| | |
|---|---|
| **1492** | Christopher Columbus reaches the Caribbean. |
| **1521** | Spanish conquest of Mexico. |
| **1534** | French explorers move into Canada. |
| **1570** | Spanish set up a colonial rule centre in Guatemala. |
| **1607** | First English colony in North America, in Virginia. |
| **1620** | Pilgrims land from the English ship *Mayflower*. |
| **1626** | Dutch found New Amsterdam, later renamed New York. |

| | |
|---|---|
| **1682** | French claim Louisiana territory. |
| **1775–83** | American Revolutionary War. |
| **1803** | USA buys Louisiana from France, doubling its size. |
| **1821** | Central American colonies break away from Spanish rule. |
| **1823** | United Provinces of Central America formed, but does not last. |
| **1840s** | Settlers and wagons move west. |
| **1848** | Gold rush in California, USA. |
| **1861–65** | American Civil War; slavery abolished in 1865. |

⬆ *The Caribbean Sea is in the Atlantic Ocean. Caribbean islands have a tropical climate. Many of the islands are formed from volcanic rock and contain vast coral reefs.*

### Where is the Panama Canal?

**The Panama Canal opened in 1914, providing a shipping short cut between the Atlantic and Pacific oceans.** The Panama Canal is 81 km long, and using it saves ships more than 12,000 km travelling around the tip of South America. The Canal was dug across the isthmus (narrow neck of land) of Panama. The area was so jungle-covered and hot that, after work started in 1881, it had to be halted after eight years because so many workers died of disease and exhaustion. The canal cuts through the continent at its narrowest part.

### How did the Caribbean Sea get its name?

**When Spanish explorers arrived in the New World from Europe in 1492 they called the sea in which they discovered the islands, 'Mar Caribe', after the Caribs who lived there.** The Caribs were Native American people who had settled on the islands we now call the 'West Indies' and on the mainland of South America (see page 26). Within a few years the Caribs were completely wiped out by wars, enforced slavery and diseases brought by the Europeans. Most Caribbeans today are the descendants of Africans and Europeans.

### How did Greenland get its name?

**When Viking sailors first saw the island, they were encouraged when they saw the green grass and so settled.** Most of Greenland today looks white, not green, because the island is almost entirely covered by ice and snow. Only the coast has a small amount of vegetation in summer. The name Greenland also encouraged others to follow and start settlements. Greenland today actually belongs to the European country of Denmark.

⬆ *Inuit people of the Arctic traditionally make ice-houses as temporary hunting lodges. They hunt and fish in the sea for food.*

| | |
|---|---|
| **1898** | Spanish–American war. |
| **1909** | Robert Peary reaches North Pole. |
| **1914** | Panama Canal is completed. |
| **1939–45** | Second World War. |
| **1948** | Organization of American States founded. |
| **1959** | Revolution in Cuba. |
| **1969** | US astronauts walk on the Moon. |
| **1979** | Rebels overthrow government in Nicaragua, leading to civil war. |
| **1991** | Collapse of Soviet Union leaves the USA as the only world superpower. |

## Amazing **facts**

- Powerful tropical storms, known as hurricanes, affect the Caribbean between May and October.

- In 1943 a new volcano appeared in Mexico. It was given the name Paricutín. Red-hot lava poured out of the ground and within one year the volcano had risen to 300 m high.

- Trinidad's Pitch Lake is strange because it doesn't contain water and it is possible for people to walk over it. The lake contains hot, sticky, black tar, which covers about 57 ha to a depth of about 40 m.

- The Caribbean islands are famous for beaches of white sand, but on the island of Montserrat they are grey, brown or black.

The fourth largest continent, South America, is almost twice as big as Canada. It has the world's largest tropical rainforest, the world's longest river, and the Andes Mountains, as well as areas of grasslands. It has a rugged, forested interior, and volcanic eruptions and earthquakes are frequent. Most South Americans are descendants of the ancient civilizations, such as Aztec and Maya, or of European, African or Asian descent. The main languages spoken on the continent are Spanish and Portuguese.

## What is Latin America?

**The name Latin America is used for Mexico, Central America and South America.** Most people living here speak Spanish or Portuguese – languages that developed in Europe from Latin. The settlers and explorers who sailed to America from the late 1400s took these languages with them, and they became widespread, although some Native American languages have survived. Many of the customs of Latin America also show signs of Spanish or Portugese influence. Many of the people, for example, are Roman Catholic Christians. European missionaries converted the local people to Christianity but some traces of pre-Christian religions remain in local customs and rituals.

## What is Argentina's biggest city?

**Argentina's biggest city is its capital, Buenos Aires.** The city has a population of more than ten million people and a very busy port. It was founded in 1536 as a port on the Rio de la Plata, and the name is spanish for 'fair winds'. Buenos Aires is famous for its broad streets and wide plazas, or squares, such as the Plaza de Mayo. Many people have moved from the countryside to live in towns or cities, such as Buenos Aires, where more employment and higher wages can be found.

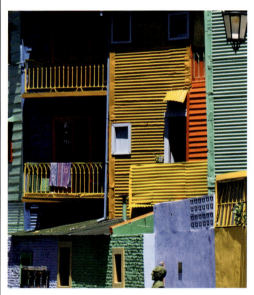

↑ *Residential districts are called barrios, and one called La Boca is noted for its colourful painted houses. Many of the city's poorest inhabitants live in shanty towns on the outskirts of the city.*

# Facts and **statistics**

## Key **dates**

**c. 10,000 BC** Hunters spread south from North America.
**c. 2600 BC** Mayan culture in Central America.
**AD 200** Nazca culture in Peru.
**1438** Inca empire in the Andes.
**1500** Pedro Cabral claims Portugal.
**1532** Spanish conquer Incas.
**1776** Spain sets up the Viceroyalty of La Plata, a colony in South America.

**1809** Wars of independence against Spanish rule in South America.
**1817** José San Martín leads an army across the Andes during wars with Spanish.
**1819** Simon Bolívar of Venezuela becomes first president of Gran Colombia.
**1821** Peru becomes independent.
**1822** Brazil becomes independent.
**1825** Bolivia declared a republic.
**1860** Argentina takes its modern name.
**1888** Slavery is abolished in Brazil.

**1889** Brazil becomes a republic.
**1898** Spanish–American War.
**1914** Panama Canal opens.
**1932–35** Bolivia and Paraguay at war.
**1959** Fidel Castro becomes Cuba's Communist leader.
**1979** Civil wars in Nicaragua and El Salvador.
**1982** Falklands War between Argentina and Britain.
**1990** Chile becomes a democracy again.

## Why do people visit Machu Picchu?

**One of the most amazing insights into South America's past is the lost city of Machu Picchu, built by the Incas in the 1400s.** The terraced city high in the Andes Mountains was one of the last refuges for the Inca people after their empire was conquered by Spain in the 1500s. It had stone houses, a royal palace and army barracks, and around it were fields cut into the mountain slopes. The city was abandoned and forgotten, until it was rediscovered by an American archaeologist in 1911.

⊕ *The ruins of Machu Picchu lie northwest of the city of Cuzco, Peru, in mountains more than 2,000 m high.*

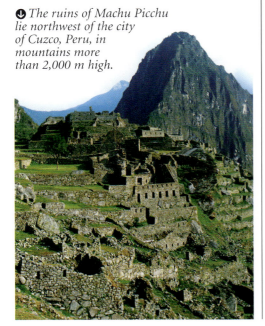

⊕ *The statue of 'Christ The Reedemer' overlooks Rio de Janeiro. Founded by the Portuguese in 1565, this Brazilian city is a busy port, famous for its music, beaches and vibrant carnivals.*

## Where do most South Americans live?

**About 75 per cent of South Americans live in cities.** Many of the cities are badly overcrowded like São Paulo in Brazil, which has some of the worst slums in the world. However, much of South America is thinly populated. Few people live in the high Andes Mountains or in the Amazon rainforest – though settlement there is being encouraged.

## Where can you see Sugar Loaf Mountain?

**Sugar Loaf is a curiously-shaped mountain overlooking Rio de Janeiro, the second biggest city in Brazil after São Paulo.** Sugar used to be sold in solid blocks of this shape. On Corcovado Mountain, another peak across Guanabara Bay, stands a 30-m statue of 'Christ The Redeemer', which can be seen from most parts of the city.

## Vital statistics

| Area | 17,871,000 sq km |
|---|---|
| Population | More than 350 million |
| Major cities | Buenos Aires (Argentina), Lima (Peru), Rio de Janeiro (Brazil), Santiago (Chile), São Paulo (Brazil) |
| Largest country | Brazil – 8,511,957 sq km |
| Highest mountain | Aconcagua, Argentina – 6,959 m |
| Longest river | Amazon River – 6,448 km |
| Largest lake | Lake Maracaibo, Venezuela – 13,511 sq km |
| Main religion | Christianity – c. 474 million |

## Amazing facts

• Not all of South America is forest or mountain. There are also vast regions of grasslands, such as the Pampas of the south and the Llanos of the north.

• Nicaragua is named after a Native American tribe called the Nicarao.

• Chile is the world's longest country, about 4,300 km from end to end.

• Balsa wood, from a tree grown in South America, is one of the lightest woods known – a third of the weight of cork.

• Brazil has one of the world's largest dams, the Itaipú, which dams the Paraná River to produce electricity.

A ustralia, New Zealand, Papua New Guinea and the Pacific island groups of Melanesia, Micronesia and Polynesia form Oceania. Australia is the world's sixth largest country and is populated by people of mostly aboriginal, European and Asian descent. It is the only country that is also a continent in its own right. To the south of Oceania lies the much bigger and uninhabitable landmass of Antarctica.

## Which country is the biggest wool producer?

**Australia produces more wool than any other country in the world.** More than one-quarter of the world's wool is shorn from sheep roaming the sheep stations (farms) of Australia. Australia has a vast and dry interior, but is also rich in pasture ideal for sheep-grazing. There are approximately 150 million sheep in Australia. Some sheep stations can reach up to 15,000 sq km in size. The sheep that produce most wool are Merino, a breed originally from Spain and able to thrive in an arid climate.

## What is it like in Antarctica?

**The ice-covered continent of Antarctica is bare and empty due to its harsh climate.** It was first seen by Captain Cook in 1773, but it was not until the 20th century that Roald Amundsen (1911) and Robert Scott (1912) reached the South Pole. In the 1950s a land expedition crossed Antarctica and today there are scientific bases used by visiting scientists to study the climate, geology and wildlife. Antarctica is protected from exploitation by an international treaty, deeming it to be a 'continent for science' only.

# Facts and statistics

## Key dates

| | |
|---|---|
| **c. 30,000 BC** | Aboriginal peoples live in Australia. |
| **c. 4000 BC** | People sail to settle Pacific islands. |
| **c. 1550 BC** | Ancestors of Polynesians arrive in west Pacific from southeast Asia. |
| **AD c. 400** | First settlers on Easter Island. |
| **c. 850** | Ancestors of Maoris reach New Zealand in canoes. |
| **1300s** | Second wave of Maoris settle in New Zealand. |

| | |
|---|---|
| **1400s** | Malay and Chinese explorers visit northern Australia. |
| **1520** | Magellan sails into the Pacific, from Europe. |
| **1606** | Dutch explorers reach Australia. |
| **1642** | Tasman explores Tasmania and New Zealand coasts. |
| **1768–71** | Cook claims New South Wales for Britain. |
| **1788** | First British settlement in Australia. |
| **1840** | New Zealand becomes British colony. |

| | |
|---|---|
| **1851** | Gold rush in Australia. |
| **1860–61** | Explorers cross Australia. |
| **1901** | The federal Commonwealth of Australia comes into being. |
| **1914–18** | Australia and New Zealand fight alongside allies in First World War. |
| **1939–45** | Australia and New Zealand fight alongside allies in Second World War. |
| **1950s** | New migration to Australia after Second World War. |
| **1990s** | Australian aboriginal land rights recognized by law. |

## Where is Polynesia?

**Polynesia is a region in the Pacific Ocean.** There are perhaps as many as 30,000 islands in the Pacific, the world's biggest ocean. The three main groups of islands are Melanesia in the west, Micronesia in the north, and Polynesia in the east. Polynesia covers the largest area – the easternmost island in Polynesia is Easter Island, which is more than 6,000 km from New Zealand.

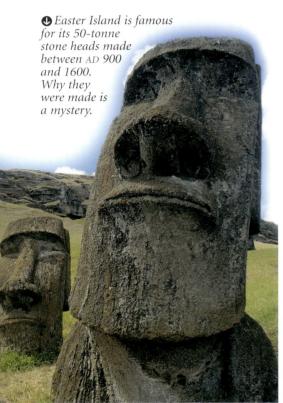

⊕ *Easter Island is famous for its 50-tonne stone heads made between AD 900 and 1600. Why they were made is a mystery.*

## What is Ayers Rock?

**Ayers Rock is a reddish sandstone landmark in Australia's Northern Territory.** It is about 2.4 km long, 1.6 km wide, and 8 km around the base. The rock rises 335 m from the sandy plain in which it stands. Aboriginal people thought the rock was sacred, and made wall paintings in caves there. Europeans first saw the rock in 1872.

## Where do people called kiwis live?

**The New Zealanders are nicknamed kiwis.** The flightless bird of New Zealand called the kiwi has become one of New Zealand's national emblems, and a friendly nickname for its people. With about 60 million sheep and eight million cattle, New Zealand is one of the major exporters of wool, meat and many dairy products. as well as the main producer of the kiwi fruit.

⊕ *The aboriginal people of Australia call Ayers Rock Uluru, which means 'great pebble'.*

⊕ *About 10 per cent of New Zealanders are Maoris, whose ancestors came from the eastern Pacific in about AD 850. The Maori culture is still very much alive in New Zealand, with their traditions and language being upheld.*

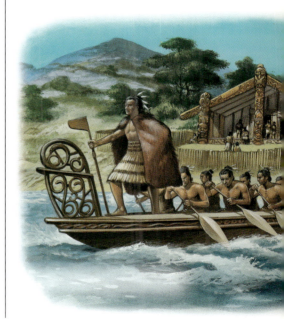

## Vital statistics: **Oceania**

| | |
|---|---|
| Area | 8,547,000 sq km |
| Population | More than 30 million |
| Major cities | Auckland (New Zealand), Melbourne (Australia), Perth (Australia), Sydney (Australia) |
| Largest country | Australia – 7,686,843 sq km |
| Highest mountain | Mount Wilhelm, Papua New Guinea – 4,509 m |
| Longest river | Murray–Darling, Australia – 2,740 km |
| Largest lake | Lake Eyre, Australia – 9,700 sq km |
| Largest desert | Australian Desert – 3.8 million sq km |
| Main religion | Christianity – *c.* 24 million |

## Vital statistics: **Antarctica**

| | |
|---|---|
| Area | 13,986,000 sq km |
| Population | Visiting scientists and tourists, but no permanent population |
| Highest point | Vinson Massif – 4,897 m |
| Thickest ice | About 4,800 m deep |
| Most active volcano | Mount Erebus – 3,794 m high |
| Dangerous hazards | Icebergs at sea, blizzards on land |
| Coldest spot | Vostok Station, a Russian base where in 1983 a record temperature of −89°C was recorded |

Every society needs a structure to make laws, defend its citizens, fix taxes and spend money for the good of all. That is why governments exist. The first governments were headed by powerful rulers, such as a king. The ancient Greeks had the first democracy – or rule by the people – though neither women nor foreigners could vote. Democracy in various forms is practiced across the world, though ideas differ as to what 'democracy' really means.

## What is the difference between a republic and a monarchy?

In a republic, a parliament or assembly are elected by members of the public who vote: in a monarchy, even though the government can still be elected, the unelected king, queen, emperor or empress is the head of state. The crown (the symbol of monarchy) is hereditary and so passes through a royal family, from parent to child. Today, they are not usually elected (though Malaysia's kings are). A president is either the head of the government (as in South Africa) or the head of state (as in France), or both. The President of the USA is head of both state and government and acts like chief executive.

*The Capitol building in Washington is the seat of the United States Congress, the law-making body for the nation. The President's home is nearby, in the White House.*

## What is a dictatorship?

A dictatorship is a type of government in which a person or group of people rules a country with absolute power. There are often no legal restrictions over a dictator's power and they govern by decree rather than by election. Dictatorships can be established through violence and maintained through physical force and a limitation of people's freedom of speech and behaviour. For example, curfews can be imposed, whereby citizens must not leave their homes after a certain time of day. Dictators often control the media, allowing only their message to be broadcast or published.

## Facts and statistics

### Key dates

**c. 3500 BC** First local governments: kings become first rulers.

**c. 3000 BC** Kings of Egypt and Chinese emperors are believed to have god-like powers.

**c. 400s BC** Greek city-states have democratic assemblies to make laws – though women are not allowed to take part.

**100 BC** Roman Empire starts to expand over much of Europe, North Africa and Middle East.

**AD 800s** In Europe, assemblies of nobles advise kings.

**1500** New ideas of the Renaissance start to challenge royal power.

**1649** English Parliament executes King Charles I.

**1776** American Revolution, leading to the creation of the United States of America (USA).

**1789** French Revolution overthrows the monarchy.

**1900s** Women in most countries win the right to vote (enfranchisement).

**1945** The United Nations (UN) is set up as an international governing body in an attempt to prevent further world war.

**2004** Enlarged European Union (EU) of 25 members has a Parliament and Courts of Justice, which can overrule some member states' laws.

## Which is the world's biggest communist country?

**China is the world's largest communist country, though in recent years it has embraced a capitalist economy.** China has had a communist government since 1949. The communist leader Mao Zedong tried to destroy 'old China' with a cultural revolution in the 1960s, but today's Chinese leaders are less revolutionary and more interested in economic growth. Communism allows only one political party, the Communist Party, and tries to control most aspects of people's lives.

*Statues in Beijing's Tiananmen Square mark the scene of a student-led pro-democracy movement in 1989, which was violently crushed by the government.*

*In a free election, such as those held in some African countries, voters mark a ballot paper, which is then put into a box. Electronic and postal voting is also sometimes allowed.*

## Why do people vote?

**People vote to elect a head of state, government or local councillor (someone to represent their views at council level).** In a democracy, people over a certain age are allowed to vote. Some non-democratic countries do not allow their citizens the right to vote: instead, these people are told who will govern them. People across the world have had to fight for their right to vote, in particular women. Known as suffragettes, women fought for equal voting rights with men and had to overcome fierce opposition in order to win. Even today many countries will not allow women to vote.

## What does a prime minister do?

**In many countries the prime minister is the head of a government but not the head of state.** He or she is usually chosen by the political party that wins a national (general) election and forms a new government. The prime minister appoints other ministers to run government departments. In Britain there is no fixed term of office for the prime minister, though a parliament must be elected at least every five years. In some countries women have only been encouraged to enter into politics at a high level relatively recently. India had a woman prime minister, Indira Ghandi, elected in 1966.

*The world's first woman prime minister was Sirimavo Bandaranaike of Sri Lanka. She first took office in 1960. Her husband had also been prime minister but was assassinated in 1959. When her daughter, Chandrika Bandaranaike, became president of Sri Lanka in 1994, she reinstated her mother as prime minister.*

*The Supreme Court, located in Washington DC, has nine judges. They rule on whether the federal, state or local governments of the nation are acting according to the Constitution of the US.*

# Amazing **facts**

- The world's biggest national assembly is China's National People's Congress. However, China is not a democracy: almost 3,000 assembly members belong to the Communist Party.

- The use of the word 'parliament' in England dates from 1241, but 400 years earlier, Saxon kings had a council of advisers, known as the witan.

- The first country in which women had the same voting rights as men was New Zealand, in 1893.

- The European Union (EU) has its own law court, and its rulings apply to all member states.

- The idea of 'one person, one vote' dates from the 1800s.

- Left-wing or socialist governments champion the good of the majority over that of the individual. At the extreme left-wing of the political spectrum is communism: shared public ownership and the means of production, distribution and exchange.

- Right-wing governments offer greater support to the individual. At the extreme right-wing of the political spectrum is fascism: a type of movement that supresses democracy and promotes the supremacy of the state over the individual. Examples of fascists are Hitler and Mussolini, who tried to create societies bred from one single race.

The world's many religions teach various beliefs about the creation of the world, the afterlife, why evil exists and good behaviour. The religions with the greatest number of followers are Christianity, Islam, Judaism, Buddhism, Confucianism, Hinduism, Shinto and Taoism. Other world religions include Sikhism, Jainism Baha'ism and Zoroastrianism.

↑ *The Wailing Wall in Jerusalem is the last remnant of the ancient Temple of Solomon, and is a special, holy place for Jews who come from across the world in order to pray there.*

## Where did Christianity begin?

Christianity is based on the life and teachings of Jesus Christ, who was born in about 4 BC in Palestine and crucified by the Roman governor of Palestine in about AD 30. Jesus' teachings were spread by his followers or disciples, who established the first Christian churches. Christianity was spread to every continent by European explorers. There are Christians across the world today and most belong to Roman Catholic, Protestant or Eastern Orthodox churches.

## Why do pilgrims travel to Mecca?

The most sacred place for Muslims is Mecca, in Saudi Arabia, because this was the birthplace of the Prophet Muhammad, who founded Islam in 622. It was from Mecca that Muhammad began his journey to Medina. Millions of Muslims travel to Mecca every year, as they are expected to make a pilgrimage, or *hajj*, once in their lifetime, if they are able.

↓ *Muslims are called to prayer from the mosque five times a day and turn to face towards Mecca as they pray.*

## Which was the first religion to teach about one God ?

The first main religion to teach that there was only one supreme God was Judaism, the religion of the Jews. Christianity and Islam are also 'monotheistic' or 'One God' faiths. Early religious beliefs were based on the worship of many nature-gods, such as the Sun, Moon, trees, rocks, and animals. The ancient Greeks had a large family of gods, headed by Zeus the King of the Gods. Hinduism too has many gods.

# World **religions**

### Big and small
Christianity is the most widespread of the world religions, with nearly two billion followers in more than 200 countries. One of the least widespread is Mandaeanism, which has about 38,000 followers in Iran and Iraq.

⊙ *The Pope is the head of the Roman Catholic Church, the largest branch of the Christian church.*

# Origins of **religion**

| Religion | Founder | Date founded |
|---|---|---|
| Buddhism | Based on the teachings of Siddhartha Gautama | c. 500 BC |
| Christianity | Based on the life and teachings of Jesus Christ | c. 30 |
| Hinduism | No known founder | c. 2500 BC |
| Islam | Prophet Muhammad | c. 610 |
| Judaism | Based on the laws of Moses and Abraham | c. 1650 BC |
| Sikhism | Guru (teacher) Nanak | c. 1480 |

⬆ *Angkor Wat has five central towers within a moated enclosure. The tallest tower is 70 m high.*

## Who was the Buddha?

**The Buddha was a prince in Nepal around 500 BC, called Siddhartha Gautama.** When he was about 30 years old, the prince became disillusioned with the material world and sought spiritual enlightenment through meditation. He travelled through India for about six years and finally attained 'enlightenment' and became known as 'Buddha', meaning 'enlightened one'. Buddha taught that by detachment from the material world and possessions, humans could achieve *nirvana*, a state of eternal peace.

## What is Angkor Wat?

**Angkor Wat is a Hindu temple built by the Khmer people, in what is now Cambodia.** Built in the early 1100s, in honour of the Hindu god Vishnu, it is the largest religious building in the world. It was also used as an observatory and later housed the tomb of the Cambodian king who commissioned the building. Though Angkor Wat was later abandoned, it was rediscovered in the 1860s by a Frenchman named Henri Mouhot and was restored by archaeologists.

➡ *Statues representing Buddha are found all over parts of Asia. These Buddha statues in Japan are made from gold-leaf.*

# Most **followers**

| | |
|---|---|
| Christianity | almost 2 billion |
| Islam | more than 1 billion |
| Hinduism | c. 800 million |
| Buddhism | c. 356 million |
| Traditional beliefs | c. 225 million |
| Sikhism | c. 23 million |
| Judaism | c. 14 million |

➡ *Sikhs have five important symbols, known as the ks. The first is kesh (uncut hair). All Sikh men have beards and wear their hair inside a cloth turban.*

⬇ *The other four ks are kaccha, kara, kirpan and kangha.*

kaccha (breeches)

kirpan (dagger)

kangha (comb)

kara (bracelet)

There are at least 4,000 languages in the world. People who speak the same languages may also share the same customs, but other customs (such as New Year or birthday celebrations) are common to people all over the world. In all human societies, people mark the seasons, growing up, and events, such as marriages and deaths, in certain ways. Each culture or group has its own festivals.

↑ *Hieroglyphs are picture symbols that represent ideas and sounds. The Egyptians used hieroglyphics for more than 3,000 years for inscriptions on temple walls.*

## How can customs change?

**Some customs and festivals are very ancient and their original meaning has sometimes been forgotten.** Hallowe'en was an ancient festival associated with the onset of winter and darkness. Medieval Christians turned it into a religious festival called All Saints' Day (November 1) and this is still celebrated by Christians in the USA and UK today. However, Hallowe'en has also become a night for young people to dress up as ghosts and play 'trick or treat'. However, in Catholic Mexico, Hallowe'en is still a religious day.`

← *The Chinese celebrate New Year in January and February with fireworks and parades by people carrying colourful dragon models. Dragons in China are associated with good luck. The Chinese calendar, used for more than 4,000 years, has years named after animals: rat, ox, tiger, rabbit/hare, dragon, snake, horse, sheep/goat, monkey, rooster, dog and boar/pig.*

## Which is the most spoken language?

**More people speak Standard Chinese or Mandarin than any other language, though the language spoken in the most countries is English.** English has spread to every continent. Languages change and grow as they are spoken and new words are added. If a language is no longer spoken, it is extinct. Latin, the language of the ancient Romans, is rarely spoken though people still study and read books that were written in it. Language originally developed very slowly from basic sounds. Grammar, vocabulary and sound-patterns all change with the structure of languages. Different languages evolve with common usage and local dialects.

## Customs and meanings

### Alphabets
The term alphabet derives from 'alpha' and 'beta', the first two letters of the Greek alphabet. The 26-letter English version of the Roman alphabet, which is what this text is written in, was continually evolving for many years before the Romans finalized it. Most English-speaking people use about 5,000 words in speech, and about 10,000 words when writing. There are more than one million words in the English language and this grows each year.

↓ *Not every word or sign can be translated. The per cent sign is universal, and so are some numbers, but Arabic, Hebrew and Chinese numbering is different.*

## Language facts

**Longest alphabet** – Cambodian (74 letters)
**Most common vowel** – a (in every known language)
**Most concise language** – Japanese (the longest word has only 12 letters)
**Most common place name** – Newton ('new town') name in English
**Word with most meanings** – 'set' (about 200)
**Most languages spoken in one country** – Papua New Guinea (more than 800 local languages)
**Longest speech** – 22 hours
**Most spoken artificial language** – Esperanto

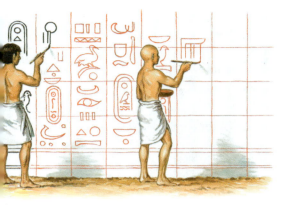

## When did people first write down words?

**The earliest known writing is Sumerian cuneiform, which dates from about 6,000 years ago.** The oldest known alphabet comes from the ancient city of Ugarit, Palestine, and dates from 1450 BC. An alphabet is a collection of letter-signs standing for the sounds we make when we speak.

## Do customs vary across the world?

**Customs vary from one country or culture to another.** In some parts of the world, such as Thailand, crossing your legs in someone's house is considered insulting. In Brazil, it is offensive to local people to make an 'o' with your thumb and forefinger – elsewhere this is a sign of satisfaction.

## Where is tea drinking a polite ceremony?

**Tea drinking is an important ceremony in Japan that is taken very seriously.** Known as 'cha-no-yu', it is a formal occasion with strict rules, often taking place in a special room. The tea is prepared using special utensils and is served in a bowl from which each guest drinks in turn. Everyone keeps very calm and still, the aim being to find beauty and meaning in simple, ordinary acts, like drinking tea.

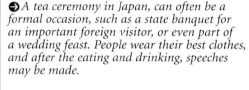

*A tea ceremony in Japan, can often be a formal occasion, such as a state banquet for an important foreign visitor, or even part of a wedding feast. People wear their best clothes, and after the eating and drinking, speeches may be made.*

## Are languages related?

**Most languages belong to families, but there are exceptions, such as Basque, which is spoken in a northern region of Spain.** Korean was once thought to be unrelated to any other language but it is often argued that it falls within the Altaic family. English evolved from the Indo-European 'parent' language and belongs to the Germanic branch of the family, along with German, Dutch and Swedish. Welsh belongs to the Celtic branch, and French and Spanish belong to the Romance branch.

# Special **days**

| Date | Celebration |
|---|---|
| 1 January | New Year's Day (except some Southeast Asian countries) |
| late Jan – mid Feb | Chinese New Year |
| 14 February | St Valentine's Day |
| 21 March | World Poetry Day |
| 22 March | World Day for Water |
| 1 April | April Fool's Day |
| 7 April | World Health Day |
| 1 May | May Day |

| Date | Celebration |
|---|---|
| 3 May | World Press Freedom Day |
| 5 June | World Environment Day |
| 20 June | World Refugee Day |
| 4 July | Independence Day (USA) |
| 14 July | Bastille Day (France) |
| 8 September | International Literacy Day |
| 21 September | International Day of Peace |
| 5 October | International Teachers' Day |
| 16 October | World Food Day |

| Date | Celebration |
|---|---|
| 24 October | United Nations' Day |
| 31 October | Hallowe'en |
| 11 November | Armistice Day |
| 20 November | Universal Children's Day |
| 2 December | International Day for the Abolition of Slavery |
| 3 December | International Day of Disabled Persons |
| 10 December | Human Rights Day |
| 25 December | Christmas Day |

Now's your chance to test your knowledge on world geography! Use this quiz to find out how much you know about continents, landmarks, government, religion and much more. This quiz will ask questions about what you have learnt from this book (grouped into subject areas as found in the book), as well as asking questions about the world that you may have studied already.

## The World

1 Which continent has more people: South America or Africa?
2 Which sea separates Europe from North Africa?
3 Is there more land or more water making up the Earth's surface?

## Asia

4 Where in China is the Forbidden City?
5 In which Asian country would you find Mount Fiji?
6 What is the modern name of Constantinople?

## Asia

7 What city houses the Temple of the Emerald Buddha?
8 What is Sri Lanka's currency: the dollar, the pound or the rupee?
9 In which country would you find the Ural Mountains?

## Africa

10 Which is South Africa's largest city?
11 Which of these countries is not in Africa: Afghanistan, Benin or Sudan?
12 Apart from Egypt, name one of the other two countries the River Nile flows through?

## Africa

13 In which ocean would you find the island of Zanzibar?
14 Kruger Park game reserve is in which African country?
15 Nairobi is the capital city of which African country?

## Europe

16 Which city is the headquarters of the International Red Cross?
17 Name the Scandinavian countries?
18 Which tiny European state holds a Grand Prix, an open tennis competition and the Rose Ball?

19 Which European country does this flag represent?

## Europe

20 In which country would you find the volcano, Mount Etna?
21 What does the abbreviation EU stand for?
22 In which European river would you find the Lorelei Rocks?

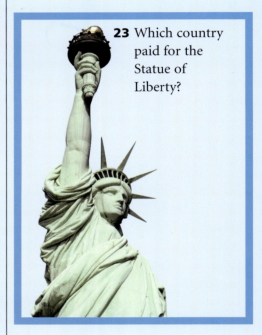

23 Which country paid for the Statue of Liberty?

## North America

24 Which waterfall is on the border between the United States and Canada?
25 Which is the highest lake in North America?
26 Alphabetically, what is the first US state?

## North America

27 Which Canadian lake, originally called Emerald Lake, lies in front of the Victoria Glacier?
28 Which is the world's largest Spanish-speaking city?
29 The Pilgrim Fathers sailed to North America from which continent?

## South America

**30** In which South American city would you find the statue of 'Christ The Redeemer'?

**31** In which South American country is Guarani spoken: Argentina, Ecuador or Paraguay?

**32** Valparaiso is in which South American country?

## Oceania and Antarctica

**33** Is Port Moresby the capital of Fiji, Papua New Guinea or Tahiti?

**34** Botany Bay is an ex-convict settlement found in which country?

**35** The All Blacks is the nickname given to which country's rugby team?

## Government

**36** Which form of government is ruled by a king or queen: republic or monarchy?

**37** Which politician lives in the White House?

**38** Which of these countries is led by a communist government: China, England or India?

**39** In which Australian city is the famous opera house?

## Religion

**40** Which city in Israel is held sacred by Jews, Muslims and Christians?

**41** The four Vedas are the oldest sacred books of which religion: Hinduism, Judaism or Buddhism?

**42** Passover is a festival in which religion?

## Languages and Customs

**43** What is the official language of Macao, Mozambique and Angola?

**44** Italian is one of the languages of the Vatican City, can you name the other?

**45** Are walloons French, Dutch or Spanish-speaking peoples?

# Answers

| | | | |
|---|---|---|---|
| 1 Africa | 13 Indian Ocean | 24 Niagara Falls | 36 Monarchy |
| 2 Mediterranean | 14 South Africa | 25 Yellowstone Lake | 37 The president of the United States |
| 3 More water | 15 Kenya | 26 Alabama | 38 China |
| 4 Beijing | 16 Geneva, Switzerland | 27 Lake Louise | 39 Sydney |
| 5 Japan | 17 Denmark, Finland, Iceland, | 28 Mexico City | 40 Jerusalem |
| 6 Istanbul | Norway and Sweden | 29 Europe | 41 Hinduism |
| 7 Bangkok | 18 Monaco | 30 Rio De Janeiro | 42 Judaism |
| 8 Rupee | 19 Bulgaria | 31 Paraguay | 43 Portuguese |
| 9 Russia | 20 Italy | 32 Chile | 44 Latin |
| 10 Johannesburg | 21 European Union | 33 Papua New Guinea | 45 French-speaking |
| 11 Afghanistan | 22 Rhine | 34 Australia | |
| 12 Sudan or Uganda | 23 France | 35 New Zealand's | |

The publishers would like to thank the following artists who have contributed to this book:
Peter Dennis, John James, Martin Sanders, Mike White

The publishers wish to thank the following sources for the photographs used in this book:
Warren Morgan/CORBIS p8 (c/l); Nik Wheeler/CORBIS p8 (t/r); David Ball/CORBIS p9 (t/r); Wally McNamee/CORBIS p10
(b/l); Alexander Nemenov/AFP/GETTY p12 (c); Gerard Vandenberghe/AFP/GETTY IMAGES p15 (c/l);
Joe McDonald/CORBIS p17 (t/l); Charles and Josette Lenars/CORBIS p17 (c/l); Roger Wood/CORBIS p17 (b/l);
Jonathan Blair/CORBIS p19 (b/l); Alan Schein/CORBIS p23 (b/r); Dennis Degnan/CORBIS p27 (t/r)

All other photographs are from:
Corel, Digital Vision, digitalSTOCK, ILN, PhotoDisc